*"Cheewa James helps us **Catch the Whisper of the Wind.**"*

— **The Taos News**

"It brings back memories of my Yuki-Little Lake grandmother, whose gentle hands raised me."

— **Darlene Brown Toyebo**, Concow, Yuki-Little Lake and Shoshone-Bannock Indian

Audio tape order:
1-800-444-2524 ext. 8

"The oral interpretation in the accompanying audio tape is done in a clear, lyrical voice...this stirring presentation can make a significant contribution..."

— **The School Library Journal**

"The music is absolutely breathtaking. It has lingered with me for days."

— **Bill Follis**, chief, Modoc Tribe of Oklahoma

Clyde "Chief" James photo: Peter Haley
Back cover photo: Ben Newbold
Cover design: Cheewa James and Annegra Hart
Page design: and layout: Cheewa James and
Annegra Hart

Catch the Whisper
of the Wind

CLYDE "CHIEF" JAMES
Modoc, 1900-1982

by Cheewa James

Published by HORIZON 2000
3330 Union Springs Way
Sacramento, CA 95827
Second Edition
First printing 1992

Library of Congress Catalog Number 93-091582

ISBN number   0-9632665-2-7

This book is dedicated to my father

Clyde "Chief" James
1900-1982

and

my two sons

David J. and Todd Easterla

The three men who have most profoundly touched my life....

Acknowledgements

Catch the Whisper of the Wind is a vision quest.

The vision is one that calls upon all people to feel the heartbeat of humanity, acknowledging the wealth and excitement of human diversity.

The quest of searching out another people's spirit and philosophy is a compelling one. Each culture offers knowledge, insight and joy.

Catch the Whisper of the Wind has been a spiritual adventure that has made friends of strangers and soulmates of friends. It has reinforced the thought that a worthy vision quest is an attraction for the positive thinkers and the givers of the world.

This is a humble undertaking. It is only a small glimpse of the sensitivity of American Indian thinking and culture. To the vision seeker, so much remains to be unveiled and pondered.

The richness of Native American culture awaits those who explore the message of this book and the accompanying narration and music.

I acknowledge the dedication, spirit and love that Annegra Hart has given to this project. She has done page layout, tapped resources and spent late night hours critiquing the music and words George and I wove.

Composer/musician George Tricomi was a delightful companion as we explored together the aura of American Indian music — and took the traditional and combined it with innovative, new compositions. He called on the sounds of many worlds and cultures to weave into his music.

What a joy it was to find Jean Villaseñor and feel the connection with her lovely spirit. In her words, "The spiritual foundation of this continent has already been laid by the American Indian."

I extend my appreciation to Naturegraph Publishers, Inc., located in Happy Camp, California, for granting permission to use the Villaseñor's works from *Indian Designs*.

Thanks to Bud Gardner for the warmth and caring of his friendship and for the support that he so willingly extended.

To my friend, photographer Peter Haley, I am grateful for the mystical picture of my father, Clyde "Chief" James, taken before my father rounded the arc in the circle of life.

Raymond Haring, with all his computer knowledge, was so helpful, particularly with the transferring of the illustrations. He, too, came under their spell.

I would like to acknowledge Darlene Brown Toyebo's friendship and encouragement. She is a special friend. My thanks also to Joan Ainslie and Paulette Kelley for their contribution of Native American quotes.

Cheewa James

Foreword

The Native American voice was once a mighty roar across this land.

But just as the vast buffalo herds once thundered across the plains and are no more, the voice of the American Indian has faded to a whisper.

The powerful voice and the age-old wisdom of the Native American — carried in drumbeat and passed from tongue to tongue as the evening fires met the twilight — still live.

The timeless philosophy and principles for living await those who choose to

— Catch the Whisper of the Wind —

What

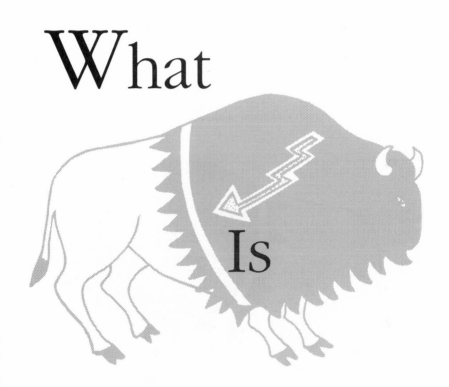

Is

Life?

What is life?

It is the flash of a firefly
in the night.

It is the breath of a buffalo
in the winter time.

It is the little shadow
which runs across the grass
and loses itself in the Sunset.

1   *— Crowfoot, Blackfoot Indian*

My heart is filled with joy
   when I see you here,
   as the brooks fill with water
   when the snow melts
   in the spring;

And I feel glad as the ponies do
   when the fresh grass starts
   in the beginning of the year...

I was born upon the prairie
   where the wind blew free
   and there was nothing to
   break the light of the sun...

Do not ask us
   to give up the buffalo
      for the sheep.

— Ten Bears, Commanche

We are part fire, and part
dream.
We are the physical
mirroring of Miaheyyun,
the Total Universe,
upon this earth,
our Mother.

We are here to experience.
We are a movement of a hand
within millions of seasons,
a wink of touching within
millions and millions
of sun fires.

And we speak
with the mirroring of the sun.

3   — *Fire Dog, Cheyenne*

Look and listen for
the welfare of the whole people
and have always in view
not only the present
but also
the coming generations,
even those whose faces
are yet beneath
the surface of the earth—
the unborn of the future Nation.

4   *—Constitution of the Five Nations*

When legends die,
there are no more dreams.

When there are no more dreams,
there is no more greatness.

5   *— anonymous*

Everything
the Power of the World does
is done in a circle.

The sky
is round, and I have
heard that the earth is round
like a ball and so are all the stars.
The wind, in its greatest power,
whirls. Birds make their nests in
circles, for theirs is the same
religion as ours. The sun
comes forth and goes
down again in a
circle. The
moon does
the same, and
both are round. Even
the seasons form a great
circle in their changing and always come back where they were.
The life of a man is a circle from
childhood to childhood, and
so it is in everything
where power
moves.

— *Black Elk, Oglala Sioux*

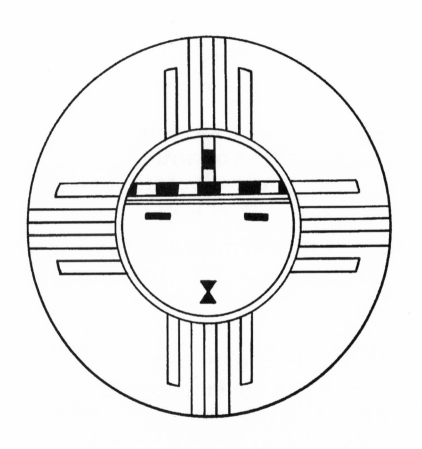

Look at your
neighbor and make him sparkle.

Your eyes
are the mirror of your soul.

When you sparkle your eyes,
whether you think
you are beautiful or not,
you are.

7   — *Twylah Nitsch, Seneca*

Wars are fought to see
who owns the land, but in
the end it possesses man. Who
dares say he owns it — is he
not buried beneath it?

8   — *Cochise, Chiricahua Apache*

I wish all to know
that I do not propose to sell
any part of my country,
nor
will I have the whites
cutting our timber
along the rivers,
more especially the oak.

I am particularly fond of the
little groves of oak trees.
I love to look at them,
because
they endure the wintry storm
and the summer's heat, and
— not unlike ourselves —
seem to flourish
by them.

9   — *Sitting Bull, Hunkpapa Sioux*

You must teach your children
    that the ground beneath
    their feet is the ashes
    of our grandfathers.

So that they will respect the land,
    tell your children that
    the earth is rich with
    the lives of our kin.

Teach your children what
    we have taught our children,
    that the earth is our mother.

Whatever befalls the Earth
    befalls the sons of the Earth.

If men spit upon the ground
    they spit upon themselves.

This we know.
    The Earth does not
    belong to man,
    man belongs to Earth.

This we know.
    All things are connected
    like the blood which
    unites one family.

All things are connected.
    Whatever befalls the Earth
    befalls the sons of the
Earth.

        Man did not weave
        the web of life;
    he is merely a strand in it.

    Whatever he does to the web,
        he does to himself.

— *Interpretation of Duwamish
                thought*

In the life of the Indian
there was only one inevitable
duty,
— the duty of prayer —
the daily recognition
of the Unseen and Eternal...
Each soul
must meet the morning sun,
the new, sweet earth, and
the Great Silence
alone.

Whenever,
in the course of the daily hunt
the red hunter comes
upon a scene
that is strikingly
beautiful or sublime

— a black thundercloud
with the rainbow's glowing arch
above the mountain,

a white waterfall
in the heart of a green gorge,

a vast prairie tinged
with the blood-red of sunset

— he pauses for an instant
in the attitude of worship.

He sees no need
for setting apart
one day in seven as a holy day,
since to him
all days are God's.

— *Ohiyesa, Santee Sioux*

Did you know that trees talk?
Well they do.

They talk to each other,
and
they'll talk to you
if
you listen...

I have learned a lot from trees:
sometimes
about the weather,
sometimes
about animals,
sometimes
about the Great Spirit.

12   — *Walking Buffalo,*
                      Canadian Stoney Indian

At the edge of the cornfield
a bird will sing with them
in the oneness of
their happiness.

So they will sing together in tune
with the universal power,
in harmony with
the one Creator
of all things.

And the bird song,
and the people's song,
and the song of life
will become one.

13— Song of the Long Hair Kachinas, Hopi

Kinship
with all creatures
of the earth, sky, and water
was a real and active principle...

And so close
did some of the Lakotas
come to their feathered and
furred friends that in
true brotherhood
they spoke
a common tongue.

The animals had rights —
the right of man's protection,
the right to live,
the right to multiply,
the right to freedom, and
the right to man's indebtedness.

14   —*Luther Standing Bear, Teton Sioux*

Animals and plants are taught
by Wakan tanka
what they are to do.

Wakan tanka
teaches the birds to make nests,
yet the nests of all birds
are not alike.

Wakan tanka
gives them merely the outline.
Some make better nests
than others...

The reason Wakan tanka
does not make two birds,
or animals,
or human beings exactly alike
is because each is placed here by
Wakan tanka
to be an independent
individuality and to rely on itself...

It is the same with
human beings;
there is some place which
is best adapted to each...

**All living creatures and all plants
are a benefit to something...**

A man ought to
desire that which is genuine
instead of that which is
artificial.

Long ago there was no such
thing as a mixture of earths
to make paint.

There were only three colors
of native earth paint
— red, white and black.
These could be obtained
only in certain places.

When other colors were desired,
the Indians mixed the
juices of plants,
but it was found
that these mixed colors faded
and it could always be told
when the red was genuine
— the red made of burned clay.

— *Okute, Teton Sioux*

The Lakota thought of air
much the same way
as the white man
does of water —
   something cleansing,
   something to bathe in.

Our bodies bathed in air, and
breathing was not only
   conducted through nose
   and lungs but with
   the entire body...

Bodies were nourished
not only by food...
   wind, rain and sun
   also nourished.

16   — *Luther Standing Bear, Lakota*

A Nation is not conquered
until the hearts of its women
are on the ground.

Then it is done,
no matter how brave its
warriors
nor how strong its weapons.

17   — *Traditional Cheyenne saying*

When you get married
do not make an idol
of the woman you marry;
do not worship her.

If you worship a woman
she will insist upon
greater and greater
worship as time goes on.

18   — *Sam Blow Snake, Winnebago*

It is not only now
that woman causes trouble.

That has been
since first man was.

19   — *Father of Thunderchild, Plains Cree*

Marriage
among my people
was like traveling in a canoe.

The man
sat in front
and paddled the canoe.

The woman
sat in the stern but
she steered.

20   — *anonymous*

I never did get a woman
        that thought the way I did.

It's like a guessing game.

If you don't
        know anything about it,
        you guess wrong
        and lose.

— *Navajo man*

It is well
to be good to women
in the strength of our manhood
because
we must sit under their hands
at both ends of our lives.

22   — *He Dog, Oglala Sioux*

Love songs
are dangerous.

If a man gets to singing them
we send for a medicine man
to treat him and
make him
stop.

23   — *anonymous, Papago*

A man
was chief only as long
as he did the will of the people.

If he got
to be too chiefy,
he'd go to sleep one night,
and wake up the next morning
to find that he was chief
all to himself.

The tribe would
move away in the night,
and they didn't wait four years
to do it, either.

— *Sun Bear, Chippewa*

Training began with children
who were taught to sit still
and enjoy it.

They were taught
to use their organs of smell,
to look when there was
apparently nothing to see,
and to listen
intently when all seemingly
was quiet.

A child that cannot sit still is a
half-developed child.

25   — *Luther Standing Bear, Lakota*

If you do bad things
    your children will follow you
        and do the same.

If you want to raise
    good children,
        be decent yourself.

26   — *In-the-Middle, Mescalero Apache*

Good acts
done for the love
of children become
stories good for the ears
of people from other bands.

They become as coveted things,
and are placed side by side
with the stories of war
achievements.

27   — *Social tradition, Assiniboine*

Do not speak of evil
   for it creates curiosity in
      the minds of the young.

28   — *Lakota proverb*

Lose your temper with a child
and you will age in sorrow.

29   — *Algonquin proverb*

Children
    must early learn the
        beauty of generosity.

They are taught to give what
    they prize most,
        that they may taste the
           happiness of giving.

The Indians in their simplicity
    literally give away
        all that they have —

    to relatives,
    to guests of other tribes
    or clans,
    but above all
    to the poor and
    the aged,

    from whom they can
    hope for no return.

30   *—Ohiyesa, Santee Sioux*

My young men
shall never work.
Men who work cannot dream;
and wisdom comes to us
in dreams.

You ask me to plow the ground.
Shall I take a knife and
tear my mother's breast?
Then when I die
she will not
take me
to her bosom
to rest.

You ask me to dig for stone.
Shall I dig under her skin
for her bones?

Then when I die I cannot
enter her body to be born again.

You ask me to cut grass and
make hay and
sell it and
be rich
like white men.
But how dare I cut off my
mother's hair?

— *Smohalla, Nez Perce*

The
man who
sat on the
ground in his tipi
meditating on life and
its meaning, accepting the
kinship of all creatures and
acknowledging unity with the
universe of things was infusing
into his being the true essence
of civilization.

32 — *Luther Standing Bear, Lakota*

We who are clay
blended by the Master Potter,
come from the kiln of Creation
in many hues.

How can people say one skin is
colored, when each has its own
coloration?

What should it matter
that one bowl is dark
and the other pale,
if each is
of good design
and serves its purpose well.

33   — *Polingaysi Qoyawayma, Hopi*

He who is present at a
wrongdoing
and lifts not a hand
to prevent it,
is as guilty
as the wrongdoers.

34

— *Estamaza, Omaha*

Even if
the heavens
were to fall on me,
I want to do what is right...
I never do wrong
without a cause.

35

— *Geronimo, Chiricahua Apache*

Let me be a free man —
   free to travel,
   free to stop,
   free to work,
   free to trade where I choose,
   free to choose
      my own teachers,
   free to follow the
      religion of my fathers,
   free to talk and think
   and act for myself —

and I will obey every law
or submit to the penalty.

36   — *Chief Joseph, Nez Perce*

The Yani Indian Ishi, America's last stoneage Indian, stepped out of his pre-history world in 1911 to be confronted with a startling, exciting, bewildering new world.

On his death, five years later, his friend Dr. Saxton Pope said:

**"He looked upon us
as sophisticated children
— smart,
but not wise.**

**We knew many things,
and much that is false.**

**He knew nature,
which is always true.**

His were the qualities of
character that last forever.

He was kind;
he had courage and self-
restraint,

and though all
had been taken from him,
there was no bitterness
in his heart.

His soul
was that of a child,
his mind that of a philosopher."

— *Dr. Saxton Pope*

Every struggle,
whether won or lost,
strengthens us for the
next to come.

It is not good for people
to have an easy life.
They become
weak and inefficient
when they cease to struggle.

Some need
a series of defeats before
developing the strength and
courage to win a victory.

38   — *Victorio, Mimbres Apache*

I will not lie to you.
I do not deceive you.
I come to lead.

39   — *Cochise, Chiricahua Apache*

Just what Power is
    I cannot explain,
        for it is beyond
            my comprehension.

Those who seek it
    go alone that
        they may be tested
            for worthiness.

It is a gift
    to be bestowed
        not only for virtue but
            for prayer and
                courage.

— Victorio, Mimbres Apache

In you,
as in all men,
are natural powers.

You have a will.
Learn to use it.
Make it work for you.

Sharpen your senses
as you sharpen your knife...

We can give you nothing.
You already possess everything
necessary to become great.

41   — *Legendary Dwarf Chief, Crow*

When you begin a great work
you can't expect to finish it
all at once; therefore,
you and your
brothers
press on,
and let nothing discourage you
till you have entirely finished
what you have begun...

Though you may hear birds
singing on this side and
that side, you must
not take notice
of that,
but hear me
when I speak to you,
and take it to heart, for you
may always depend
that what I say
shall be true.

42 — *Teedyuscung, Delaware*

You must speak straight
so that your words may go
as sunlight into
our hearts.

43   —*Cochise, Chiricahua Apache*

As a man is
climbing up he
does something
that marks a place
in his life where the
powers have given him
the opportunity to express
in acts his peculiar endowments,

so this
place, this act,
forms a stage in
his career, and he
takes a new name to
indicate that he is on a
level different from that
which he occupied previously.
Some men can rise only a little
way, others live on a dead level.

Men having power to advance,
climb step by step.

44 — *The Kurahus Tahirussawichi, Pawnee*

The Indian believes
profoundly in silence —
the sign of a perfect
equilibrium.

Silence is the
absolute poise or
balance of body,
mind and spirit.

The man who preserves
his selfhood is ever calm
and unshaken by the
storms of existence...

What are the fruits of silence?
They are self-control,
true courage or
endurance, patience,
dignity, and reverence.

Silence is the
cornerstone of character.

— *Ohiyesa, Santee Sioux*

Peace...
comes within the souls of men
when they realize their
relationship, their oneness,
with the universe

and
all its powers,

and
when they realize that
at the center of the Universe
dwells Wankan tanka,

and
that this center
is really everywhere.
It is
within each of us.

46   *— Black Elk, Oglala Sioux*

Have patience.
   All things change
      in due time.

Wishing cannot
   bring autumn glory or
      cause winter to cease.

47   — *Ginaly-li, Cherokee*

The longer a problem
   is allowed to exist,
      the harder it is to
         return to peace of mind.

48   — *Twylah Nitsch, Seneca*

The selfish man is lonely, and
his untended fire dies.

49   — *Pima man*

Free yourself
from negative influence.
Negative thoughts are the old
habits that gnaw at the roots
of the soul.

50   — *Moses Shongo, Seneca*

A brave man dies but once —
cowards are always dying.

51   — *Moanahonga, Iowa*

One has to face fear
or forever run from it.

52 — *Hawk, Crow*

Do not judge
your neighbor until
you walk two moons in
his moccasins.

53 — *Northern Cheyenne proverb*

Kindness
is to use one's will
to guard one's speech and
conduct so as not to injure
anyone.

54 — *Omaha oral tradition*

Lose your temper
and you lose a friend;

Lie and you lose yourself.

55   *— Hopi proverb*

To be lazy
    while there is plenty
        means death
            when there is little.

56   *— Winnebago proverb*

Do not stop watering the corn
while you count on
the clouds to
bring rain.

57 — *Dan George*

The Ute who follows two rabbits
will perhaps catch one,
and often none.

58 — *Dan George*

Honor age!
Even an old blind man
may guide you to
a rainbow.

59   — *Micmac proverb*

No one likes to be criticized,
but criticism
can be something
like the desert wind that,
in whipping the tender corn
stalks, forces them to strike
their roots down deeper for
security.

60   — *Polingaysi Qoyawayma, Hopi*

My father sent for me.

I saw he was dying.
I took his hand in mine...
He said: "Always remember
that your father
never sold his country...

   Never forget my dying words.
      This country holds your
         father's body.

   Never sell the bones of your
      father and your mother..."

I buried him in that beautiful
valley of winding waters.
I love that land more than
all the rest of the world.

      A man who would
   not love his father's grave
   is worse than a wild animal.

We live, we die,
and,
like the grass and trees,
renew ourselves
from the soft clods of the grave.

Stones crumble and decay,
faiths grow old
and they are forgotten,
but new beliefs are born.

The faith of the villages
is dust now,
but
it will grow
again like the trees.

— *Old One, Wanapum*

A few
more passing suns
will see us here no more, and
our dust and bones will mingle
with these same prairies.

I see
as in a vision the
dying spark of our council fires,
the ashes cold and white.

I see
no longer the curling smoke
rising from our lodge poles.

I hear
no longer the songs
of the women
as they prepare the meal.

The antelope have gone;
the buffalo wallows are empty.

Only the wail of the
coyote is heard.

The white man's medicine
is stronger than ours;
his iron horse rushes over
the buffalo trail.

He talks to us
through his 'whispering spirit'
(the telephone).

We are like birds with
a broken wing.
My heart is cold within me.
My eyes are growing dim —

I am old....

— *Chief Plenty-Coups, Crow*

A single twig breaks,
but the bundle of
twigs is strong.
Someday I
will embrace
our brother
tribes and
draw them
into a bundle
and together we
will win our country
back from the whites.

— *Tecumseh, Shawnee*

We respected our old people
above all others in the tribe.

To live to be so old
they must have been brave
and strong,
and good fighters,
and we aspired to be like them.

We never allowed our old people
to want for anything...

We looked upon our old people
as demigods of a kind,
and we loved them deeply.
They were all our fathers.

65   — *Buffalo Child Long Lance, Sioux*

There was a time when our
people covered the land as the
waves of a wind-ruffled sea
cover its shell-paved floor.
But that time long since
passed... Our people are
ebbing away like a
rapidly receding
tide that will
never return...

Tribe follows tribe, and nation
follows nation, like the waves of
the sea. It is the order of nature,
and regret is useless.

Your time of decay may be distant
but it will certainly come for
even the White Man, whose
God walked and talked
with him as friend
with friend, cannot be
exempt from the
common destiny.

We may be brothers after all.
We will see...

Even the rocks which seem to be
dumb and dead as they swelter
in the sun along the silent
shore thrill with memories
of stirring events connected with the lives of my
people, and the very
dust upon which
you now stand

responds more lovingly to their
footsteps than to yours because it
is rich with the dust of our
ancestors, and our bare feet are
conscious of the sympathetic
touch...

And when the last Red Man shall
have perished and the memory
of my tribe shall have become a myth among the
white man these shores
will swarm with the
invisible dead of
my tribe,

and when your children's
children think themselves
alone in the fields,
the store,
the shop,
upon the highway
or in the silence of the
pathless woods, they will not
be alone...

At night when the streets of your
villages and cities are silent and
you think them deserted they
will throng with the returning
hosts that once filled them and
still love this beautiful land.

The White Man
will never be alone.
Let him be just and
deal kindly with my people
for the dead are not powerless.

Death — I say?
There is no death.
Only a change of worlds.

66   — *Interpretation of Duwamish*
thought

Mother Corn
has fed you, as she has fed
all Hopi people,
since long, long ago
when she was no larger
than my thumb.

Mother Corn
is a promise of food and life.
I grind with gratitude
for the richness of
our harvest,
not with cross feelings
of working too hard.

As I kneel at my grinding stone,
I bow my head in prayer,
thanking the great forces
for provision.

I have received much.

I am willing to
give much in return...
there must be a giving back
for what one receives.

— *Sevenka Qoyawayma, Hopi*

Old age
was simply
a delightful time,
when the old people sat
playing in the sun
with the children
until they
fell asleep.

At last, they failed to wake up.

68   *— Jaytiamo, Acoma*

Oh the comfort,
the inexpressible comfort
of feeling safe with a person,
having neither to
weigh thought
nor
measure words,

but
pouring them all right out,
just as they are,
chaff and grain together,
certain that
a faithful hand
will take and
sift them,
keep
what is worth keeping,
and with a breath of kindness,
blow the rest away.

— *anonymous, Shoshone*

The old people came literally to
love the soil
and they sat
or reclined
on the ground
with a feeling of being close to a
mothering power.

It was good for the skin to touch
the earth,
and the old people
liked to remove
their moccasins and walk with
bare feet on the sacred earth.

Their tipis were built upon the
            earth and their altars
                    were made of earth.

The birds that flew in the air
            came to rest
                    upon the earth,
                            and it was the final
abiding place of all things that
            lived and grew.

The soul was soothing,
            strengthening,
                    cleansing,
                            and healing.

This is why the old Indian
    still sits upon
        the earth
            instead of propping
himself up and away
    from its life-giving forces.

For him, to sit or lie
    upon the ground
        is to be able to think
            more deeply
and to feel more keenly.

He can see more clearly
    into the mysteries of life
        and come closer in
kinship to other lives about him.

— *Chief Luther Standing Bear, Teton Sioux*

70

**It
does
not
require
many words
to speak the truth.**

71

— Chief Joseph, Nez Perce

It was chiefly owing
to their deep contemplation
in their silent retreats in the
days of youth
that the old Indian orators
acquired the habit of carefully
arranging their thoughts.

They listened
to the warbling of birds
and noted the grandeur
and the beauties of the forest.

The majestic clouds
— which appear like mountains
of granite floating in the air —,
the golden tints
of a summer evening sky,
and all the changes of nature,
possessed
a mysterious significance.

72 — *Francis Assikinack (Blackbird) Ottawa*

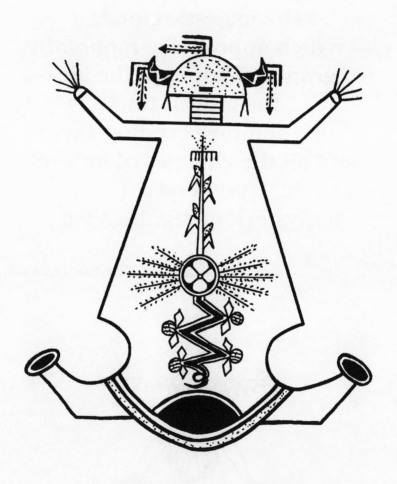

There will be happiness
before us.
There will be happiness
behind us.
There shall be happiness
above us.
There shall be happiness
below us.
There shall be happiness all
around us.
Words of happiness shall extend
from our mouths.
For we are the essence of life.

73   —*Navajo Prayer Ending*

Which of these is the
wisest and happiest —
he who labors without ceasing
and only obtains,
with great trouble,
enough to live on,
or he who rests in comfort
and finds all that he needs
in the pleasure of hunting and
fishing?

74   *— Micmac Chief (1676)*

We first knew you as
a feeble plant
which wanted a little earth
whereon to grow.
We gave it to you.

And afterward, when we could
have trod you under our feet, we
watered and protected you.

And now you have grown
to be a mighty tree,
whose top reaches the clouds,
and whose branches
overspread the whole land,
whilst we, who were the tall pine
of the forest,
have become a feeble plant
and need your protection.

75   — *Red Jacket, Seneca*

Look at me —
I am poor and naked,
but I am the chief of the nation.
We do not want riches,
but we do want to train
our children right.
Riches would do us no good.
We could not take them with us
to the other world.
We do not want riches.
We want peace and love.

76 — *Red Cloud, Sioux*

Why should you take by force
that from us
which you can have by love?

77 — *Powhatan, Powhatan*

To be a great people is not just
to be fine hunters
and famous warriors.
The Great Spirit thinks it is far
more important for us
to be good and kind
to one another, so that we don't
look down on other people, but
help them with love and
understanding.

78   — Sweet Medicine, Cheyenne

A people without a history is
like wind on the buffalo grass.

79   — *Teton Sioux proverb*

Father, I love your daughter,
will you give her to me,
that the small roots of her heart
may entangle with mine —
so that the strongest wind that
blows shall never separate them.

It is true I love him only,
whose heart is like the sweet juice
that runs from the sugar-tree
and is brother to the aspen leaf,
that always lives and shivers.

80   — *Anonymous, Canadian*

...It may be thought that the memory of things may be lost with us. We nevertheless have methods of transmitting from father to son an account of all these things. You will find the remembrance of them is faithfully preserved, and our succeeding generations are made acquainted with what has passed, that it may not be forgot as long as the earth remains.

81

— *Kanickhungo, Iroquois*

Your
mind must be
like a tipi. Leave
the entrance flap open so
that the fresh air can enter and
clear out the smoke of confusion.

82 — *Chiefeagle, Teton Sioux*

My heart laughs with
joy because I am
in your presence....
Ah, how much more
beautiful is the sun today
than when you
were angry with us!

83 — *Chitmachas Chief*

If all would talk
and then do as you have done,
the sun of peace
would shine forever.

84 — *Satank, Kiowa*

What! Would you wish that
there should be
no dried trees in the woods and
no dead branches on a tree
that is growing old.

85

— *Huron*

꒱꒱꒱꒱꒱꒱꒱꒱

Do not grieve.
Misfortunes will happen to the
wisest and best of men.
Death will come, always out of
season.
It is the command of the Great
Spirit, and all nations and people
must obey.
What is past and what cannot be
prevented
should not be grieved for....
Misfortunes do not flourish
particularly
in our lives —
they grow everywhere.

86

— *Big Elk, Omaha*

You must not hurt anybody
or do harm to anyone.
You must not fight.
Do right always.
It will give you satisfaction
in life.

87 — *Wovoka, Paiute*

The path to glory is rough, and
many gloomy hours
obscure it.

88 — *Black Hawk, Sauk*

It is not necessary for eagles to
be crows.

89 — *Sitting Bull, Teton Sioux*

I think you had better put the
Indians on wheels so you
can run them about
wherever you wish.

90 — *anonymous*

The Great Spirit made the world
to always change,
so birds and animals can move
and always have green grass and
ripe berries,
sunlight to work and play,
and night to sleep;
summer for flowers to bloom,
and winter for them to sleep;
always changing;
everything for good;
nothing for nothing.

91   *— Flying Hawk, Oglala Sioux*

Everyone can be happy,
even the most insignificant
can have his song
of thanks.

92   *— Pawnee*

**When your time
comes to die,
be not like those
whose hearts are filled with the
fear of death;
when their time
comes, they weep
and pray for a little more time
to live their lives over again
in a different way.**

**Sing your death song,
and die like a hero going home.**

93   *— Tecumseh, Shawnee*

All life was injustice....
Lightning
found the good man and the bad;
sickness carried
no respect for virtue,
and luck flitted around like the
spring butterfly.
It is good to learn this
in the days
of the mother's milk.

94

— *Bad Arm, Sioux*

Death cannot be helped.
It is ever thus.
Do not look
where you have come from,
but rather look
forward
to where you are to go.

95

— *Zuni widow*

We shall not long
occupy much room in living;

the single tree
of the thousands which sheltered
our forefathers —
one old elm under which the
representatives of the tribes were
wont to meet —
will cover us all;

but we would have our bodies
twined in death among its roots,
on the very soil
on whence it grows.

— Wa-o-wo-wa-no-onk, Cayuga

The Modoc guns are sure.
The Modoc heart is strong.
But hear me,
oh muck-a-lux (my people)!

The white men are many.
They will come again.
No matter how many
the Modocs kill,
more will come.

We will all be killed in the end.

97   *— Keintepoos (Captain Jack), Modoc,
during the Modoc War of 1872-73*

May serenity circle
on silent wings
and catch
the whisper of the wind.

— *Cheewa James, Modoc*

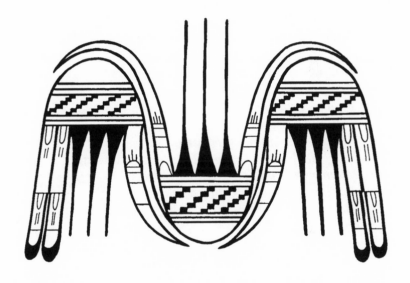

Illustrations

Illustrations in book, correlated by number to text

1 - *Pueblo Buffalo*

2 - *Acoma Pueblo Bird*

6 & 10 - *Pueblo Sun Symbols* - The sun is the emissary of the Great Spirit, without which all life on Earth would perish.

11 - *Pueblo Eagle* - The eagle is a lofty concept, denoting inspiration, ideals and courage.

14 - *Santa Domingo Pueblo*

16 - *Isleta Pueblo Rain Bird*

17 - *Pueblo pottery of the Rio Grande* - symbolic of the paradoxical world in which we live

19 - *Hohokam Bird* - ancient

20 - *Acoma Pueblo design*

24 - *Pueblo Owl Design*

27 - *Pueblo Grasshopper*

30 - *Apache Ceremonial Figure*

31 - *Zia Pueblo Dragonfly* - the spirit of growth
Miembres Catfish - ancient pottery design

34 - *Pueblo Cricket Design* - ancient

37 - *Hopi Rain Bird Spirit* - A vortex of energy: the spirit of creation is incorporated in all the elements which bring forth life.

45 - *Pueblo Bear* - powerful symbol of strength

51 - *Pueblo Turtle Design*

57 - *Acoma Pueblo Water Bird*

61 - *Isleta Pueblo Fish*

62 - *Papago Indian Design*

63 - *HORIZON 2000 logo* (publisher of — *Catch the Whisper of the Wind* —)
Hohokam Load Carrier - ancient 1000-1200 A.D.

66 - *Zia Pueblo Dragonfly* - the spirit of growth

69 - *Miembres Deer* - ancient design

70 - *Acoma Pueblo Pigeon*

71 - *Hopi Sun and Cloud Kachina* - given to little girls for good behavior: bringers of sunshine

72 - *Zuni Bird Woman*
   Zuni Bird Man
73 - *Mother Earth* - Navajo
74 - *Father Sky* - Navajo
75 - *Miembres Ram* - ancient
76 - *Acoma Pueblo Bird*
77 - *Miembres Bird (1000 A.D.)*
78 - *Acoma Water Bird*
79 - *Gambel Quail* - from Hohokam pottery 1000 A.D.
80 - *Aztec Codices* - from *The Book of the Aztec*
81 - *Aztec Codices* - from *The Book of the Aztec*
82 - *San Ildefonso Bird*
91 - *Santa Domingo Pueblo Goat*
93 - *Miembres Pueblo Turkey*
94 - *Acoma Quail*
98 - *Hopi Rain Bird Spirit* - bringing abundance to
   the earth

Narration

The audio cassette tape available with this book has selected writings narrated by Cheewa James. The selections are framed in traditional Native American melodies, accented with innovative new sounds from composer George Tricomi.

Narration number from the book and corresponding first line:

1 - What is life?
2 - My heart is filled with joy
3 - We are part fire, and part dream
6 - Everything the power of the world does
8 - Wars are fought to see
10 - The Earth does not belong to man (last part)
12 - Did you know that trees talk
14 - At the edge of the cornfield
17 - A nation is not conquered
18 - When you get married
19 - It is not only now
20 - Marriage among my people
21 - I never did get a woman
22 - It is well to be good
23 - Love songs
25 - Training began with children
26 - If you do bad things
27 - Good acts done
28 - Do not speak of evil
29 - Lose your temper with a child
33 - We who are clay
34 - He who is present
35 - Even if the heavens
37 - He (Ishi) looked upon us
38 - Every struggle

39 - I will not lie to you
41 - In you as in all men
45 - The Indian believes
47 - Have patience
48 - The longer a problem
49 - The selfish man is lonely
50 - Free yourself
51 - A brave man dies
52 - One has to face fear
53 - Do not judge
54 - Kindness
55 - Lose your temper
56 - To be lazy
57 - Do not stop watering the corn
58 - The Ute who follows two rabbits
59 - Honor age
60 - No one likes to be criticized
62 - We live, we die
63 - A few more passing suns
64 - A single twig breaks
65 - We respected our old people
66 - There was a time when
67 - Mother corn
70 - May serenity circle

The tape is part of a
book/audio cassette album
and can be ordered with credit card:

800-444-2524 ext. 8
Fax 813-753-9396

May the spirit
of the American Indian
give you insight,
strength
and joy.

American Indian Thought

There is no such thing as an American Indian. Rather, there is a collection of people divided into separate groups, nations or tribes that is classified as "American Indian" or "Native American."

Yet for all the cultural differences in language, religion, crafts, philosophies and living habits, there are some common threads of thinking among most American Indian groups. They have been reflected in the quotations and philosophies you have read in *Catch the Whisper of the Wind*.

- ° A reverence for the environment

- ° An emphasis on and love for family

- ° A value placed on silence, personal truth, introspection and "questing"

- ° A respect for older people

- ° An acceptance of death as part of the natural order of life

- ° An acknowledgement of the value of each human being and the belief that we are all related

Catch the Whisper of the Wind
Order Form

Book — 128 pages   **$11.95**

Book and 60-minute audio cassette in beautiful gift album—uses the rhythmic pulse of Native American music in a brilliant adaptation of original compostion. Combined with the crystal clarity of Cheewa's singing and the haunting quality of her narration, this is a stunning tribute to the American Indian culture.

$21.95

— Credit card —

Order Toll-free **ANY-TIME 800-444-2524 Ext. 8**
FAX 813-753-9396

BookWorld
1933 Whitfield Loop, Suite 300
Sarasota, Florida 34243